ONCE I WAS A STONE

ONCE I WAS A STONE

Emilie Lygren

WAYFARER BOOKS
ABIQUIU, NEW MEXICO

WWW.WAYFARERBOOKS.ORG

Published in 2025 by Wayfarer Books
Cover Design and Interior Design by Connor Wolfe
TRADE PAPERBACK
978-1-965320-74-7

10 9 8 7 6 5 4 3 2 1

Look for our titles in paperback, ebook, and audiobook wherever books are sold.
Wholesale offerings for retailers available through Ingram.

Wayfarer Books is committed to ecological stewardship.
We greatly value the natural environment and invest in conservation.

ORDERS@WAYFARERBOOKS.ORG
WAYFARERBOOKS.ORG & WAYFARERMAGAZINE.COM

DEDICATION

To my nonbinary, genderqueer, and gender nonconforming
siblings
past
present
future

like the leaves, the air, the ocean
we've always been here
our existence is enduring

these poems are for you.

Table of Contents

III.

invocation

I am boy
I am girl
I am river
gone glimmer at sunrise
gone cottonwood cloud in summer
gone fishtail in the current
gone rush at the surface
gone frost heave in the chest
gone silver sagebrush in the rain

gone
some people wish I were gone
like clean air gone
like hope for rain this year gone

this euphoric explosion
of gender
uncontained
fearless
reliable
don't let it scare you

I am
not boy
not girl
just river
glimmer
gone

I.

"Do you wish you were born a boy?"
"No, I wish I was born a river."
Pınar Sinopoulos-Lloyd

A body finds its home in the sand.
All sand is a body broken.

All sand is a body broken

Where my old self was
lives a chasm.
A song.
A rusted bell.
Afternoon wind
swelling around oceans,
oaks, invisible wind chimes.

Sometimes the lines write
themselves from inside.
Sometimes the poems
laze in like horses
back from pasture.
Ring from memory
like sand crushing itself
into jewels at the coast.

Sometimes I forget
sand had to break
to become so soft.
How the sweet hiss of waves
comes from their leaving.

Sediment

outcrop (geology): a rock formation visible on the surface of the Earth

contact (geology): the surface along which one rock type touches another

On the road
I traveled every day to
get to school,
there's an outcrop.
A contact.
A cliff wall.

On one side,
flat chalkstone layers
stack themselves like books.
On the other, round,
smooth granite rocks conglomerate,
forever embedded in mud.
They rise together above asphalt.

In my dreams
I'm the mountain
every time.

I'm the crack in those
two songs of stone.
I'm boy and girl
and all the mud
in between.
Smashed together over eons.
I'm not a boy and not a girl,
just a mountain facing the sun.

These words
are my outcrop.
I'm letting you see me.
I've uncovered
myself for you.

Gathering stones

I.

As a child I gathered stones.
Black-flecked granite grown
orb-like in a stream under cottonwoods,
their durable stories,
shoved into the pockets
of my jean shorts or overalls.

When the other kids
looked at me sideways,
asked me why I didn't like
wearing dresses,
I could touch the stone
remember the trees,
who never asked me to
explain myself,
who understood
my silence perfectly.

I felt more like rock
than girl or boy,
more like sand than child,
something shaped slowly over years,
rubbed softly until smooth,

companion of tree roots,
young dragonflies,
the shimmer of fish.
When raised brows
said I didn't fit in
I wanted to stare back
solid as the stones.
Eyes winking like flakes
of mica lodged between quartz.
Just as sure of myself
as something millions
of years old, just as
unconfused.

II.
My friend's four-year-old
looks down at her new dress and says,
"This dress doesn't have pockets...*yet*."
She wants her mother to sew pockets
onto any garment that doesn't have them
so she can gather stones and feathers,
acorns, tiny bird skeletons, leaves,
things she might find along a forest path.

"Yet" works like that:
a waiting pocket.

Placeholder for the number to be solved.
Orange flags to show the line of an unbuilt roof.

And gathering works like that, too:
looking around for what shines.
How everything I have ever picked up
helped me know myself a little better.

Like the stones I held tight,
not yet knowing how sure
I would someday become.

How I wanted to be beautiful

Leaping with arms raised
to save a goal.
Standing firm and tall
at first base.
Moving a cleat through
the red infield dirt.
Pressing the spiked sole
into soft soil and seeing
divots look back at me.
Proof I could make a mark.

I didn't want to be a boy
but I wanted
to be treated like one.
Bolt of thunder
free from hairclips,
dresses and dolls.
Pride for what I did
and not how I looked.

I didn't feel like a girl either.
I felt like one of the murky-rooted cottonwoods
at the edge of the creek,
a lake shining in sunrise,
air just above an oak at the crest of a hill.

Shimmering, I pulled up my roots
every morning. Put on t-shirts
and went to school.

Later came the trying to fit in.
Slicked-back hair and low-cut shirts.
Wanting to be beautiful and chosen.

But early on I knew the best
beauty came among
trees and green rivers
and no need to be
seen as anything
but a body among bodies,
no thought towards
what I wore or who saw.

Throughout this article I will use the following words interchangeably

(you may read the poem in any direction)

gender	anemone	slither	boy
stone	river	ember	sagebrush
girl	wave	ocean	riparian
whelk	chrysalis	stone	chaparral
this	body	lives	forever

Dress up

I.

I never wanted
to be the princess.

Playing pretend
in imaginary castles,
only a knight would do.
If I closed my eyes I could
feel a horse rise beneath me,
hear the clang of swords,
my destiny wrapped
sure as cloth around the hilt.

II.

My character was a man
in the 8th grade school play.
I wore an old blue blazer
with tall shoulder pads,
a felt hat to hide my hair.

I put on my costume at home
so I could ride to school
wearing the creased pants
and brown leather shoes.

Everyone else dressed behind stage
ten minutes before the show
while I walked around feeling right.

III.
In college I wore a suit to a party,
tucked my hair under
another brown felt hat.
Outside the door
I saw friend and she jumped
when I called her by name.
She hadn't recognized me
under the sharp vest and trousers.

But I recognized myself
in that slanty body,
strutting confidently
under the melting streetlights
into the dusk.

Kindergarten

Small red rectangles on the rug
marked where we could sit,
how to organize our bouncy bodies.
We got a scissors driver's license
once we learned to cut
clean lines.

At lunchtime
in the cinderblock-bound
sand-filled playground,
we climbed on a metal
drainage pipe once painted
a faint shade of orange.

One day a boy fell off the top
and onto the sand, then lay still.
As we gathered around him
he whispered,
"I broke my back."

The other kids ran for the teacher
and I stood there stumbling for the first time
over the idea that sometimes,
people lie to get attention.

We were forbidden from climbing after that.

Most days my body felt far away.
Anxiety was a thick tar on my tongue.

Some of the best times
were when the floods came
and I stayed home
all day in the rain.

When you are alone on the schoolyard, adults tend to worry

Fall is coming but I'm not afraid.
Gone are those early school days
when I was a confused jumble
of arms, legs, words
I didn't know what to do with.
My classmates bored me
with their talk of
popular TV shows,
or teased and pushed
when teachers looked away.

I swung alone
from the metal bars
in the playground
and liked it that way.
Studied the mounds of sand
surrounded by cinderblocks,
the shadows of the oaks playing on the wall.

Listen, I thought these things were beautiful.
I smiled at the sky.

The adults thought because I was alone,
I was sad.
I wasn't.

I was in love with the light,
leaves shook down from branches,
barnacles and acorns,
the idea of whales.

I whispered about this
to the clouds and the grass,
who understood me perfectly,
who never made me feel ashamed.

Recess memory, first grade

If boys could marry boys, and you could get married twice,
I would marry you and Forrest.

He said it hugging his two best friends,
who were also in my class that year,
while I bounced a red rubber ball
on playground paint a few feet away
in the thick September heat,
the air smelling of oaks and fresh pencils,
and I remember looking at them
and feeling a small voice rise inside me
like a soft balloon—

Why not?
Why couldn't you marry them both?

And listen, it wasn't a thought borne from role models,
not in my early 90's half rancher half hippie
coastal town where almost no one came out until they left,

but was a thought instead from a voice I've learned to follow
even when no one else seems to hear it yet,
the part of me that could see no reason why

they couldn't all marry each other,
      (even with the rules against it)
the voice that knew, even then,
that it was all just a ruse.

By graduation the boys had
tallened, tattooed themselves with homophobia,
learned to stomp on softness with worn leather boots.

But in first grade they just wanted to love each other,
and I still can't see anything wrong with it,
and in the folds of my memory
I have almost nothing left from that year
except the three boys, who are still hugging,
but this time I'm pelting them with rice
and flower petals, this time I'm shouting

    Why not? Why not love them all?

What do you mean nonbinary?

Sometimes I feel like wearing a dress
and letting my curls fall in neat-messy lines
and sometimes it only feels right to wear t-shirts,
buttoned flannel shirts,
tuck my hair into a soft beige cap.

Yes I am a woman
and I also often feel ungendered.

Not between as in the middle,
or going from one place to another
but between as its own country,
kaleidoscope of color
so much broader than the polarity
of pastel blue-and-pink baby bonnets.
Between as in the place of
  yes, and,
  ungendered, fluid,
until the world
shows me I appear female,
  says I am less deserving of professional attention,
  sweeps over me like dust under a rug,
  catcalls me and expects a smile.

I am not confused.

It is actually quite simple.

Joyful, even.

The more I live into it, the more clear I feel.

But my word processing program automatically corrected
ungendered to *endangered*,
and I still think about
the first-ever compliment a boy gave me,
I was in second grade,
it was the one day I wore a skirt all year,
brown corduroy with a purple and yellow-flowered shirt,
I had brushed my hair,
and as we waited to file into the classroom after recess he said
You look nice today, Emilie. At least, nicer than you did
yesterday.
And even then I found the comment
to be fantastically funny,
and the only confusing part was the empty replay of prescribed roles,
and somehow I knew not to be hurt,
knew I was so much bigger
even though I didn't yet have the words to say how.

Book of Records

In elementary school the kids in my class made up records on the
playground:

> *the first person to sing the ABC's while playing hopscotch*
> *the highest climbed in a tree while carrying a ribbon*
> *the longest walked on the curb without falling off*
> *the most hair clips attached to a pinkie*
> *the farthest snapped rubber band.*

Everyone jumped rope frantically,
raced down the slide, dug deep in the sand
trying to be *the most* and *the best* and *the first*.

I wish someone had pulled
the competition from us,
taken us softly by the shoulders
and whispered what the years of age would reveal:
that being the only one of you,
everything you do makes history,
so you'd better try and be kind,

that you are the first at anything you try
and also the last, and every moment you remember this
tastes a little sweeter and more precarious,
like the sun dancing off your shoelaces
the first time you knotted them all by yourself.

The First Lost Tooth

The first one came out
in a buzzy restaurant.
I was eating spaghetti
tossed in olive oil
tasting of smoke.
The adults celebrated, clapped,
slipped a silver dollar
under the pillow.

With no more rocky tooth
in its socket, my mouth felt lonely.
Someone told me I could whistle
through the gap in the front
of my mouth, and I tried,
but the air only ever sounded like air
and my tongue ran over and over
the empty hole.

Flag

after "Lesson" by Rick Benjamin

I never liked it.
Not even in kindergarten.
Being asked
for allegiance
each morning.
It felt like
a prayer towards
something false and massive,
ghost too old to know
its own name.

So I hovered my hand
just above my chest,
refused to touch my heart,
didn't speak
when certain words
went by like "indivisible,"
and "under God."

But enough people droned on
that the teacher
didn't seem to notice,
and neither did the flag

inert and oblivious
against the wall
humming along,
thinking it spoke
for everyone.

Learning to fish

Round wet eye
not made for blinking.
Amber body twisting
in the mesh net.

I held the handle
as you writhed.

I put you back.
You swam away
into the current
like a slick comma.
I wished I'd never caught you,
never took anything at all.

Life history

I wanted to write but the words were too fast to hold. Poems kite-leapt quick out of my eye sockets. Wind-thrushed out of my ears. Slipped out under my fingernails. Before I could catch them. Before I could tell them to wait. Before

 I was an adult tree I was a seed. A seed everyone thought was a girl. A smart girl, a good girl who wrote in neat lines. A girl who needed some help conquering unkempt hair. Everywhere on the playground, in the neat rows of desks: girl, girl, girl. Was the only other option other than boy. And I wasn't boy like I wasn't window or wasn't freight train or wasn't sandcastle. And no one ever asked so I never got to tell them that I wasn't girl but was alder leaf, was granite stone, was cedar seed, was nighthawk. So I just wore them each day: the sash that said "girl" and frilled in the wind. The sash that said "good." Even though they never fit. Even though the words became too heavy to breathe in. I was given the sashes before I learned to speak. By an opposite fairy-godmother. By a blank-faced man in a cold suit. Told to never take them off or some part of me would die. Told to do my girl-chores, brush my hair before I could go out and play with mud and spiders. Before I could leave the house or go to school. Before

I was the pretend girl I was a river stone. Before I was not a boy my body lay thick and right and immoveable. My mind dropped thousands of words into the current. Poems zooming past. Bubbles in the drink. All too fast to hold. But their speed didn't matter. That's where home was. Under alder and cottonwood. Nestled in quartz sand. Before I learned to speak there were so many words. Before

Strand line

Old selves
are easy to break.
Toddler toys strewn
around the room
like dry seaweed,
fiercely clumped
in early autumn.

What time looks like
after school, laughter
under fuzzy stars,
adolescent fires
and songs at midnight,
trees limbless
burned after flame.

Summer is a flag
stuck in mid-wave
and part of me
is ghost-like,
quick to crack
like eggs.

I only taste
your dry ghost.
Feather boa
stripped of fluff,
once thick and oceanic
now dry walrus whiskers,
traveled from far away.

Once I was a stone along the river (Duplex)

Once I was a stone along the river.
The current always sang loudest at midnight.

    We were still singing at midnight when
    a fairy tale bell rang and we disappeared.

Every fairy tale has a disappearance.
The characters I loved never came back.

    Sometimes we love what can't come back.
    Easier to grieve than stay and rub each other to the bone.

We sanded each other's bones until we found grief.
Every day gone farther I feel the line go slack.

    Lines slacken until we are left with dust.
    Rain curls dust into swishing songs outside the window.

The rain outside turned your name into a grief song.
Some storms pull every stone from the river.

Genius loci

If I were born anyplace else
maybe I wouldn't have struggled so much
If it were another decade or century
maybe I would have known myself sooner.

But then I would not have learned to
speak from the stones, would not have
studied patience with the alder roots,
would not have first fallen in love
with changing leaves of cottonwoods,

would not have become the rainclouds
each winter, patient as the drops
pattering on the roof,
full as the silence that comes after.

Camouflage

Like a school of fish at sea
or stars melting into dawn
like the gray moths who flat
themselves against bark

I can blend so hard I disappear
let dresses of soft fabric
swoosh around my knees
hair grown long like lichen
dripping off trees

The world says "girl"
and I don't talk back
just fade into the flock.

Not today's prey
but at a cost:

    I'm safe
but unseen

Alterations

The new bathing suit
was too tight,
grasped at my chest
with underwire.
Metal meant to cause
a pleasing shape
pushed my breath
into an urgent coil.

I cut the neon fabric
and slid out two
steel half-circles.
They clattered
on the counter
and my chest expanded
and I breathed out
corsets and whale bone,
velvet and lace.

Most days, it's like this:
quietly slipping out
of what doesn't fit.
When I'm called "miss"
on the phone

or a stranger says
I am a "lovely woman,"
I smile, sidestep the words, wink
to the squeamish feeling.

Sometimes it's easier to wear
what's given instead
of explaining why
it doesn't fit.

I wish I could tell you
how big it is beyond
the two poles,
the tightly knit binary.

Inside I am ocean,
silver sagebrush drenched
in rain, wind pushing
through outstretched arms,
smooth white granite
held close by river and mud.

What we wear, nothing
but disguise. Listen long
enough and every single
thing is too tight.

Chrysalis

One day the caterpillar forms a chrysalis,
waits a while, becomes butterfly.

They told us this much, told us to wait
for chitin to split, for the emergence
of dazzling colors and pumping wings.

But they never talked about
what really happened inside:
how the caterpillar's whole body
                    dissolves,
how for a time
there is nothing but soupy liquid,
butterfly goo, formless but for the
rigid purse holding it in midair.

And no one told us, either,
that when the caterpillar was born,
while it grew and crawled along,
a few cells called *imaginal*
already held instructions for what to build
when it came time for another body.
Here, the shining eye, the scaled wings.

Let me remind you about
the power of sticking around.

If you feel shapeless and scared,
imagine yourself in that tiny,
thin-walled shell, whistling in the dark,
some part of you already knowing the way.

II.

Where my old self was
lies a chasm of
rusted understanding.

Every day something new

Even on the drabbest of mornings I hope for it:
To notice atoms arranged differently.
For something I've walked past
a hundred times
to unfold itself anew:

the way seed pods move up the stems of the toothwort.
A hummingbird catching flies in a swift arc.
New ferns greener with young growth.
The pace of the clanking flagpoles on a windy day.
The purpling of spent shooting star flowers.
Even the sound of my own thoughts rubbing against
the most familiar neighborhood street signs.

Each day a self
I've never met before
glows inside my ribs.
It's there when
I open myself to the sweet orb
of attention.
If I look.
If I listen.

The scientist and the poet

I watch a squirrel dig up
an acorn from the
vegetable garden, then
carry it away in her mouth.

Both scientist and poet
watch her furred body
coil along the fence line,
see the long tail flick
back and forth for balance,
wonder what the slick
cylindrical seed feels like
under tooth and tongue
and consider how acorns
and squirrels need one another
the way pulley needs rope,
imagine where the squirrel
might go next.

What else gets buried
and pulled back up
in a cloak of earth?

Fascination quickly
dream-cords its way
up to the clouds.

The sun's magnetic
sway speaks to seeds
under the surface.

The language of
green cell splitting
into green cell
worthy of a thousand
questions, odes, love letters
written on paper pressed
from the very same blade.

On attention

A tree stump large enough
to lay across still reaches
its muscled trunk into the ground.
I can see the knuckles of bark
inching outward, count the
hundreds of rings stilled
where a saw sliced through.
Wonder when the heartwood
cracked. Watch wolf spiders
dart in and out of the canyons
and crevasses. Study a single veined
termite wing laced with dew.
Watch a dragonfly land
and cast a shadow.
Feel the wood still damp
from last night's rain.
Smell the sawdust chewed
by beetles, changing form.

And suddenly, it doesn't
matter what I do next.
For a moment, I'm the dot
marked on the map, the
circle filled in and singing—
         you are here.

Meditation, weeds

I didn't know—
could never know
how the weeds I liked least,
maroon-stemmed
with gangly yellow flowers,
would flutter open
into a hundred soft-seeded orbs,
rising above the heads of the grass,
shimmering the light like little lamps,
whispering softly in the dusk.

I didn't know—
but could believe
how the sweet peas I planted
with so much care never germinated.
Not even one radicle sprout
shifted the surface of the soil.
My disappointment buried
with dormant seeds.

Each spring I wait and see what rises.
What's planted and planned
rarely turns up what I thought.

The seeds I hoped on stuck
under some firm mystery.
What caught my disdain
sometimes shifting
into handfuls of brittle stars,
a song I learn by heart,
look forward to each year.

Changing the daisies

Cut a daisy, then place it in water and food coloring to produce flowers of a shade similar to the dye. — Instructions for Dyeing Flower Petals, Perennial Summer Daisy Seed Packet

I put nine pale daisies
in a clear glass vase,
add a few drops of blue
dye to the water.
Hours later,
green stemmed daisies with pale blue petals
sit in afternoon light on the windowsill.
The breeze sighs:

> *Don't we all take up and hold*
> *what is in the water?*

I cannot live in the world
without saying that
how we speak to one
another matters.

I cannot live in the world
without asking for more
champions of kindness.

I cannot live in the world
and pretend it is
perennial summer—
that everything is fixed while
so many are floodstained by fear, are
clipped by the hot blade of rage.

If you think it empty

If you think the desert is empty
look close at the ground.
Small footprints, lines of sand
mark where life has been
or water flowed.

Insects stitch their flight
around creosote.
Butterflies blink
from flower to flower.
Stones make their slow
descent to sand.

Around all that space,
wind and birdsong whisper,
gain in volume the longer you stay.

If you think yourself empty,
sit. Wait for quiet.

When the wise lizard of your mind
pokes its head from the cave,
don't chase it away.

Let it wander.
Follow the tracks.

Insights from Arthropods

Sometimes all it takes
is another living thing
to ease judgment on myself.

Sometimes it's a crawdad
crawling across
slick white granite
next to a river.

Velvet body and jointed legs
skittering on shining rock
above a crushing waterfall.

I can see where
it will struggle,
where the sides
are too steep to climb.
the swift current,
the easy route one foot over.

How often I act like
I know what's coming.
Pretend the future
is a language

I know how to speak,
but still, move forward
wary and scared:
 just in case, I'll head in claws-first.

What if, like the crawdad,
I trusted this tiny inch of sight
was enough to go on,
tried to remember
that's all I've ever had.

Horsepower

how rich it must have seemed:
twenty horses pulling
eighty legs thundering inside
a closed engine whirring with oil,
spitting gravel and smoke
instead of hot mist from the nostrils
a wheel to turn instead of bit and thread

how sick it is:
to reduce an animal
to what it can do or how hard it can pull
but that's what we usually mean by *power* isn't it.
the part we call *worth* that can *do* or *make*
rent from the rest of the body—

　　　the thick mane,
　　　shining hair slipping over muscle,
　　　horse mind full of wisdom
　　　we only glimpse.

Rorschach Test, Mount Tamalpais

Some insist, from far away,
she looks like woman sleeping.

In the clear slip of morning, she's
large enough to hear Pacific waves slow and slick at Stinson,
see ferry wakes slap against rocks in Corte Madera.

How do you see her?

What can you do to the Earth when you call her a woman?
allowed to be ravaged while the Sun, a man,
floats too far and too bright to touch.
Moon, woman again but only men have
left boot marks upon her soil.

Back on the mountain, roadcuts
split down her sides and moonlight
glances off the rocks,
rumples waves at midnight.
Plants are cut bare so we have
places to step.

In summer, she holds her foggy skirts close
over sagebrush and chaparral,

and if everyone looked at me like that I would too.
Just another girl in the shape of conquest.

No mind for her multitudes:
the million ants climbing in the soil,
the tanoaks heavy with seeds,
the creeks lilting in winter,
the mountain, needing nothing like a name.

The dark-stained ink blots not a shape
but a mirror. Look at her:
your unrequested desire
throating you like a bear,
ringing your broken doorbell,
revealing your deepest lie.

The sparrows (Once again, I was wrong)

Once again, I was wrong.
And didn't even realize
I thought I was right.

Just looked at the weeds'
sharp heads and assumed
no one would want to eat them
pulled the plants by the roots
across half the garden
as the spring sun went down.

The next morning,
striped sparrows
flushed through the yard.
Clipped seed heads
by the base, swallowed whole
their three-inch spines.

Maybe I don't need to say it but I will:

how many times this happens each day,
what I think I know painting itself
across the ceiling of my mind,
furrowing the skyline,
tinting the window glass.

And how many times
I don't see the sparrow,
miss the contradiction,
look past the world glancing back,
whispering defiantly:
> *think again.*

Sheltered

When we were ten years old,
we built shelters
on a field trip to the woods.

Stacked sticks in straight lines.
Bent ferns over the top.
Flaked red bark beneath our feet.

When we finished, keyholes of light
twisted through gaps in the doorway
but we pretended not to see.
It was easy to imagine walls
nothing could move through.

We called it
     our house.
No one asked us to consider
whose land we really stood on.
They told us that we were learning survival.

We weren't.

Instead we learned
another ploy:

to take.
To build a blind,
ignore the flaws,
close our eyes to the holes
we put there.

A Reckoning with Johnny Appleseed

It sounds nice, doesn't it, walking with a bag of seeds,
papering each village with a nursery of sweet orbs,
leaving behind something that will grow and grow.

Years after I heard the name in elementary school,
I'm questioning him.
They told us he was tall and had a long beard.
I wish they'd asked us to go a little deeper.
> *What is the impact of apples?*
> *What relationships have they formed*
> *with insects and birds and people?*
> *Who planted the trees in your neighborhood?*

Johnny returned to every stand of trees he planted,
came back every two years to check up on them.

But along the way he converted Native Americans to Christianity
and planted dogfennel too, which spread West and ran wild as a
weed, just another good green thing gone mad with power.

The article on the internet told me the Native Americans thought
Johnny was touched by a Great Spirit, but I want to know what
else they said.

I've done it too, of course, thought I had something good to give
and maybe some of it was, but planted it in the ground before
asking what was there first, or what might grow instead.

I hope he put his palms to the soil and listened.
I hope he asked permission before speaking psalms.

This is what I'm trying to do with everyone who came before me.
The heroes from history class.
The ancestors I know about and the ones I don't.

Questioning the seeds they planted with good intentions.
Looking at the grown trees and the shape of their shadows.
Teasing apart the weeds from what's sweet and round.
Wondering what to put in my bag and carry on,
what to uproot, what to leave behind.

Turtles at the Convention Center

*"Texas residents have been rescuing thousands of cold-
stunned turtles amid the state's deep freeze, taking them to the
South Padre Island Convention Center."*

—Texas Newspaper, February 2021

I.

No one will have
ever so thoroughly
studied the ugly carpet.

They are unimpressed by
the automatic projector screen,
a hundred pitchers of iced tea.

They see the failing
of so many rows
of chairs that all
face the same direction.

I worry for them,
stunned by cold
in unfamiliar waters,

Where do we swim
in this blinding ocean
of artificial light?
Where we come from,
you can always follow
the sun upwards to breathe.

I feel that way too.
Not so far from an animal,
I get lost quickly anywhere indoors
without windows.

    II.
I have heard them compare
Mitch McConnell to a turtle.

I firmly believe
this is an insult to turtles.

Their shelled bodies
mostly unchanged,
a resilient frame to ride through
a hundred million years.

Age and wrinkled skin
are no failing,
but greed is.

Maybe we'd be better off
if we each lived inside
a small domed house,
need carried close to our bodies,
no space to take
anything that isn't ours.

After the second Blue Origin Spaceflight Capsule landed in the desert

Jeff Bezos paid
no attention
to the earthly creosote
when he opened the spaceship door.
Plants that clone themselves outward
in rings over millennia flurry
into yellow flowers filled
with small bees each springtime.

The Blue Origin crashed
down on desert crust,
another thousand-year threading of soil
and mycelium, algae, cyanobacteria.

Let me tell you about the dry river washes
who hold fan-shaped alluvium
from the last rain, birds who build nests
inside forests of cactus needles,
beetles who cross hot sand on tiptoe.

Jeff Bezos wore a blue suit and dead eyes.
He sprayed the riders with champagne.
He dropped the bottle, mostly full.

He dropped it while looking right at the camera.
He did not set it down for later.
He did not glance to see where it fell.
He dropped it.
Another green object
among the disposable plants.

I don't remember what anyone said about the rocket flight
or what the Earth looked like from far away.
I just remember the bottle.

For the love of spiders

Today, pulling weeds in the garden,
I saw a spider whose
abdomen and head and legs
were bright green,
the same shade of plant
I'd just wrested from the ground.

I let out a little gasp
as the wind pressed through
the grass's spindled seed heads
and I felt a familiar wonder
bloom within me, the thought
    I have NEVER seen this before,
which comes if I move slowly enough
to let myself get drenched in surprise,

and suddenly the spider became
all the things I don't know yet,
climbing the wooden fences
at the edge of my brain,
woven so delicately with mystery,
poise, dew just after rain.

And I thought of all the
photos of spiders
that friends and neighbors
have shared on Facebook and Nextdoor:
>   *Look at what I found in my house,*
>   *what should I do with it?*

The commenters always have the same chorus:
>   *Kill it! It's definitely a Brown Recluse!*
while my scientist friend and I patiently
ask them not to,
point out at least 5 observable differences
between their spider and the Recluse,
explain that there are over 3,000
species of spiders in North America
and Recluses don't even live in this part of California,
tell them
>   *it's probably a Callobium*
who are so fond of wandering inside come autumn,
resist giving a lecture on how
when you say "probably"
in science it means you're actually pretty damn sure
but want to leave some room in case you're wrong.

And I thought   *there it is again*—
how easily we press danger
on the innocent, on what we don't know.
How many people have been killed
for looking like a threat
when they had done nothing wrong,
when they were just existing in their body,
how quickly suspicion rises when
we're not curious enough.
The swiftness with which
we reach for hate.
How the gun is grasped
before one word is spoken.

How the first sentence of
every Google search preview
about every kind of spider says
whether it is venomous or not.

I, who have loved spiders since I was 10,
looked for them everywhere,
studied their webs in wonder,
am asking you to move more slowly.

I want every person you ever meet
to wear a necklace engraved with the words

You have never seen me before, take tender care.
I want to replace all of the sentences
about all spiders with that sentence.
I want the message to look you right in the face
so you remember to treat everyone like something
bright and green and new,
worthy of your slow attention.

Even the spider at the corner of your closet.
Even someone you were told to fear.
Even your best friend or aging mother,
who you think you know
but have never actually seen before
as they are on *this* spring day,
so full of pollen and dew.

Science Lesson, 5th grade

On the whiteboard:
a paper cut-out flower
cartoonish with oversized
petals and parts.

On the desks:
notebooks under fluorescent lights
labeled with definitions
       petals, anther, stamen, sepal.
Whiteboard image copied
line for line.

Just outside:
spring speaks
in hundred different colors.
Lupine, monkeyflower, poppy.
Ceanothus and columbine.
Blinking at the classroom window.

Around the flowers:
fuzzy bees and angular butterflies
sift from blossom to blossom,
faces yellow and dusty,
pressed in close.

This pencil is a lifesaving device

There are days
I think my poems would
be ashamed of me.

When fear and scarcity claw
thick at the throat, judgement
adorning my insides
with apathy and eyeroll.

Days when
I cannot summon
a single spark of wonder,
or remember
ever doing so.

The dry grass, bobbing
its seeded heads,
only a worry.
The slick dishes
waiting to be lifted
from the drying rack,
only a future chore.

But sometimes, I can
pick up my pencil and feel
the beginnings of beauty
slide a lens under my eyelids,
pull my gaze back
into soft attention:

to the moment where
the grass simply exists,
another wiry, riddled thing
breathing the foggy air,

where the dishes,
glazed and proud,
start trembling in
their wire lines,
not questioning their cyclical lives,
just grateful to be of use.

III.

"The heart that breaks open can contain the whole universe."

— Joanna Macy

Smooth stones have lost a thousand edges.
Sometimes I forget they had break to become so soft.
The broken parts are called sand,
not weakness.

III

Autumn

and I'm singing
change songs.

Sun churns leaf, roof,
chair shadow in doorway.

Small birds born tiny
and featherless last spring
fly against scattered clouds.

Once-flowers are pouches of seeds
split quick across damp ground.

Rough rocks wait quiet under earth
for rain to curl through,
sift their bodies into smooth orbs.

I sit, watching fire burn low,
winter a whisper
against slick, wet trees.

Feeding a rose to my goat

A friend told me
       goats love roses,
so I picked one
and held it out
to our white goat
at the edge of dusk.

Shy and slow,
she opened her teeth and nibbled,
swallowed the sweet-smelling,
cantaloupe-colored petals.

Some might call it waste—
to take a thing of beauty
and make it disappear from the light.

But some might call it magic—
the rose, once so still,
becoming a goat,
weaving into her cells,
being breathed out,
turning back into air.

Shelter in Place

Now is the time to look closer.
Hours we spent going somewhere
become a stare towards the wall.

Outside, rainclouds rush
past, float away to places
I cannot follow.

I start to look around the house
as if it were a museum:
the mess, intentional somehow,
alchemy in the pile of clothes,
patterns in the stacks of papers,
the chagrin of dust in the corners
a riddle before a chore.

The light sliding past the windows
never got so much attention.
Even the paper hinge of the egg carton
seems a small miracle now.

Spring planting

I spill from my hand
a dormant constellation.
Hard-capped miracles.

Where the seeds fall
and take root
a song will grow
and hold the light.

Under the earth
a soft meshed universe
weaves into itself,
knits a fertile yarn.

In a matter of weeks
I'll be able to touch
the soft leaves,
push my face
into the forest of stems,
thank each bud,
a cup to grow another
handful of stars.

The year we cut the plums

they had thrust tall,
straight branches
high into the air.
We sawed them into poles,
lay them next to the spring tufts
of dandelion and dew.

In each tree, an arbor.
Plum trees. How they multiply
their toughness.
Put your ear to the blossoms
and how you'll hear
their rushing growth.

Learning to Pray

I never asked god
for anything.
I learned to want
could be worked
towards.
Prayer for shiny hair,
for feeble excuses
confused me.

The poppy is a likeness.
Spring a question
in her opened face.
She doesn't
ask for radiance
just shines thick
enough for bees to
throb at.

Prayer stopped
on my ancestor's
lips a few links
back and there is
no one left to ask why.

I'm told they didn't speak of
god just of morals and soil.

Now I'm left
godless but
with plenty
to believe in.
Poppies leap
out of my throat.
I believe at their
feet,
their roots,
long and carrot-light.

I believe in
how seeds want
only what can be
worked toward.
To go split-husk,
to feel rain,
grow taller.

I look out at the thick
poppy field.
Whisper, to their
orange faces:

Are you there, god?

Don't tell anyone,
I'm looking
for you.

Mist prayer

Tonight I'm grateful for fog.
Thick and gray, mottling the hills,
helping the fire lie down.

The first place I love
burned twelve years ago.

Sagebrush, Sycamore, Yerba Santa.
Chaparral cragged to sharp
Central Coast mountains.
Bay, Alder, Cottonwood.
Trees grown before rain shadow.
Rivers I drank from,
rivers I floated down
now drowned in
ash and soot.

A year after the fire
I bought a small sculpture.
Blued copper nailed
to smooth umber wood,
Made from the metal melted roof
of a burned house.

Living among fire means scrambling
to patch together remnants.
Stitching glass and burnt embers.
A blanket that's never done.

Early summer rain

You might not even call it rain
but I knew it was coming before it began
when the hill across the valley softened
into mist like a picture through old glass

It was a damp curtain, barely enough to slick
the ground but still enough to pull the birds
out from tree trunks to the tips of branches,
to coat the redwoods in a layer of shine,
to cool my face and dampen my early robe.

It was enough in the middle of the deepest drought
in a thousand years to let me breathe
for a moment, to pause and count
all the things that at least,
for one morning, wouldn't burn.

Defensible space

I beg for rain—
who doesn't
when grass fires
stand up fast as sight
under breath from sitting engines,
greased rags,
the whispering of stones.

My house is stucco-hewn,
a builder's alchemy:
cement, sand, water, lime,
covering the wood,
hard and rippled,
unlikely to catch flame.

The trees are so far away I
have to walk for 26 seconds
out the door
before I can touch one.
Yes I counted, and it's
why we moved here,

for space,
for cement and stucco,
for few plants,
        no matter how we love them,
all in hopes we won't burn.

Do you see how easy it is,
how sometimes necessary?

Instead of running from threat
or even desire, to just

harden yourself,
paint something stiff
on the heart walls,
build a moat of asphalt
around your truer self,

step away from sparks, from fire,
        no matter how you love them,
better hard than burnt,
better stone than ash.

Morning meditation

A poppy closes
tightly against
the empty house.
Water wheel
slung silent.

No sun yet,
just film of clouds.
Like Earth carried
shiny and sleight
in a crinkled plastic bag.

Soon we will
all be covered in it:
Plastic beads slipping
through the bloodstream.
Plastic island
destination weddings.

I'm speaking to you
through mouthfuls of plastic.
Throaty and parched.

Unable to drink with a gullet
filled like a vacuum bag.
Seam split and steamed shut.

Water drowns
in a limber petroleum ocean.
Plastic cup-shaped
in a past life can no
longer hold liquid.

Now we're steeped in old rain
and algae and nothing potable.
Hills gone bright over creek run dry.

Even the poppies
plastic at the roots.

My anxiety goes for a walk
around the garden

wondering where the weeds will grow
and how long it will take to pull them.

I know, I know.
How much I could look at instead:

an oak leaf flushed with tiny eggs,
the bee ambling through rosemary,
spiderwebs shining at the corner of the gate.
My own thoughts about any of this.

How fast worry pushes in.
How practiced I've grown
in searching for what
could go wrong.

I steel myself against it.
Heart clenched inside
like a forgotten brick
left under the porch:

useful once,
now only a shadow,
heavy and alone.

Object Permanence

When my partner
brought home
a terrarium of roly-polies
I peeked in, worrying
when I saw
nothing moving.

How do you know
they're still in there?
I asked.

> *You can check,*
> *lift the little stick,*
> *you'll see them.*

This mantle of fear
is my inheritance.
Let me look
to make sure
you are still there
and breathing.

The sparrow
with its quick

contact chirp
in the brush.
Mother, father, friend.
Fearing the roll call
gone silent.
Lid slapped shut
before last reply.

No stomach for
Schrodinger's uncertainty,
I want everything
to sing back—

still here, still here.

Sleeping Through the Alarm

I've never done it but I have dreamed it:
a jolt through the body
eyelids whipping back,
sight and sleep come too close together.

Fear surging the quick
collection of clothes and imagined apology
about the missed appointment.

But this is not the worst thing that could happen,
nowhere close.

The dreams come too, hiding in the walls,
scarcely breathing, waiting for floorboards
to stop creaking before daring to emerge.

Under both dreams, a voice deep in the body:

> *Something is coming.*
> *You must stop it.*

> *To stop it,*
> *you must never stop*
> *yourself.*

Raincloud

After "Espenbaum" by Paul Celan

Cobblestones collect cracks and water after rain.
My namesake left before the war.

Gray bark streaks umber under clouds.
Plain brown dress, what did you pack, what was left behind?

Gray ship meets fogged skies. Like so many,
you spanned oceans: shine on, sweet prow.

New streets under black boot heels.
This is where your thread drops.

Forgotten lives float here like ochre orbs.
Your husband, useful, you, never named.

Wishing for the songs of my people (prayer for anti-appropriation)

Let me tell you what I'm looking for:

A skein of dyed wool.
A recipe for preserved meat.
Practices I can grip
from the roots.

Songs sung around solstice time,
stories woven from so many seasons in one place.
Flags of bright-patterned fabric
from before the spangled banner.

My father's father left the fjords
to become a soldier.
I was told he only ate eggs
on the train from New York to Seattle.
It was the only word
he was sure of in English.

He became American
but still longed for salty fish.

All the questions I never got to ask
hover in the evening air.

I wish he could tell me about
the tall fields of summer grain
what he knew of farming,
what seeds he stitched
into rows each spring,
what songs our ancestors sang
when they went out to fish,
whether he liked the sound of wool
spinning into yarn.

I'm looking for a scrap of cloth
to hang in the window
without stealing
from anybody.

Taking out the trash at my grandparent's house

Last week she remembered who I was.
Asked me about my writing.
Laughed about how
the teddy bears she used to sew
for children in shelters
always ended up looking
a bit strange but sweet at the same time.

In the hospital, leg broken,
her dementia put spiders on the ceiling,
sent strangers to the door.

Today I drive down the road to her house
to roll the trash cans back into the garage.
Outside the door, I stare
at the smooth stone Buddha statue,
the metal doorstop in the shape of a dog,
a pot of red geraniums
my grandfather once sat by and pruned,
the Meyer lemon tree that flowered all year
and how he'd always insist I take the fruit.

He gave me his gardening
tools once he got too weak
to walk to his community plot.
I still have the clippers and the trowel
but after he died
it took me years to throw away
the wire-woven basket, crushed on one side,
with no space to carry anything anymore.

Like refusing to set down the memory
of his tall frame leaning down to pick tomatoes,
of my grandmother's lumpy sewing,
of the three of us looking out the window
at the trees laden with pink flowers
and wondering together
when the rain would cease.

Settling the Estate

Childhood wounds reopened.
Roles reenacted:
> protector, jester, stone.

Playground power wielded with a steel voice.
Hurts pressed so far back into the chest
the tears seem to come from behind.

There are things to divide that cannot be cut
into pieces like the last slice of cake.

What was once a tumble
of limbs and laughter
shared rooms and secrets
whispered over the bedspread
has become a chasm.

Each holds a thin rope just long enough to settle the distance.
No one wants to throw first.

Grief song

Everything passes the window
just as it used to.

Unopened packages
weep at the doorway.

Their addressee's name
is stuck in your throat.

Chess pieces
frozen to the board.

Hasty autumn shadows
across black squares.

The name you chose
now lives on a gravestone.

No more neat rows.
No more moves to make.

Soil in the bottom of the flowerpot

Something holds up
the dirt surface we see,
substrate for plant roots reaching down.

But without ripping
the plant away or digging down,
can we really know?

The bottom of the flowerpot
could contain old coins,
secret notes written on old envelopes,
a sleeping squirrel, the sound of an arrow.
Whale teeth, sugar, enemy, heavy nothing.

Like the cat that flicks
in and out of being,
can we trust anything
hidden still exists?

Even the rice
you just placed
in the pantry,
even the ardent promise,
even someone

you spoke to yesterday
whose body
will never again
respond to their name.

After days of deep grief

the air feels like ocean.
But no amount of swimming lessons
readied you for this fall beyond sight.

You try to leave the house
without ripping open.
Walk the dog.
Send mail.

But everything is a trip wire
reminder of what has been lost.

The broccoli—
what you coaxed him towards as a child.
An orange— he ate so many.
Model airplanes and finger paints.

His favorite kind of bread
lines up in neat rows
at the grocery store.

One whole row
has been removed.

At the back of the shelf,
bread bags fall into one another,
barely propped up,
shaped around emptiness.

Your hand will never stop reaching
toward what he loved.
The empty row will never be refilled.
A space you'll keep stumbling over
with heart and eyes.

Hands that want
to busy themselves,
send a letter,
twist over
and over
on the heavy shore.

Death found me like a knave

after "Because I did not stop for death" by Emily Dickinson

Death found me like a knave
upon the rattle of a train
a clouded door flew open
while dirt inhaled the rain.

I joined the roots and battles
under sullen earth where worms
wove slyly up my arms
mycelium a wedding gown

my hair wrapped up in pearly cloth
my flesh turned right to air
under tooth of beetle, body
gone in sweet and soft decay.

I'm dead like dirt, dead like rain,
dead like a finished song—
which is to say in essence
I'm not dead,
not at all.

Wishes for life after death

When crows bray into caverns
and sediment slips in the rain,
when street signs falter and
the rusted gate leans from its hinges,

when I quicken from my body
like brisk night over
last warm autumn days,

look for me inside
the descending
wrentit song.
Underneath soft
granite stones.
In the yellow-turned
cottonwood corridors,
branches of purpling oaks.

I will be every raindrop
landing its ripple song
in the tumble silt
surface of the river
shuddering along alder ways.
I will be a lilt of sagebrush

silvered in clear drops
cragged on coastal hills.
I will be the pause between
every sea foam hush of each wave.

I will be embirdened,
slick seagull,
swivel head nestled
between pointed wings.
I will look down at a
sea rock clattered with
dusk light, matted
with dry grass.

Then will be the rock
looking back,
licked by blue swell
after blue swell,
unmoving, content,
striving for nothing.

Writing about my gender on a rainy winter morning, age 34

Again I'm an element.
Inside I hold canyons
and meadows, cottonwoods,
a slinging creek
full of soft stones.
I feel myself rise
with the scent of
rosemary on warm
winter days.
Finally I have
words big enough
to sweep at that feeling.

I'm out late dancing
beyond the binaries.
Fluid like rain slipping
past the window.

I float back to cloud,
change form again
and again. All dove gullet,
creek hush, lupine flower.

Picture books glow at me
through bookstore windows.
Purple covers and rainbows
and a kid in a t-shirt and tall hair
stretches their arms toward me.
 don't need to know
their name or gender to
see we're headed somewhere.

I wear whatever suits me
as long as I can still
run up the nearest mountain.
I emerge from the trees
and shimmer into the world of people.
My arms wide with unconfusion.
Legs strong and feet hugging ground
and I know exactly what I am.

Listen, it is the most joyful thing.

Mother's Day

The runner bean I planted at dusk
formed tight coils of vine by morning,
green circles grasping a nearby pole
like a newborn's firm-handed grip.

A parent's sturdy arm says
"I am here
 to help you grow.
Reach around me,
and follow me up.
This way, this way."

In time, the bean plant grows
and tops the pole.
Unfolding a hundred
broad leaves she says,

"Look, I found the light.
It is here,
and here,
and here."

112

The oldest lobster fisher in the world says she might as well keep doing it

For Virginia Oliver, age 103

The boat may fiddle and drift a bit nowadays
as it carves into the silver lines of the marsh.
Fishing for 95 years has leathered her hands, but she's
undaunted by the skirmish of wire traps and sodden ropes,
still loves the hush of reeds in the breeze,
tells time by the clink of the ship's bell.

I stare at the unweeded garden
and think about all I have not kept doing.
What I walked away from as a child because
I couldn't stand being bad at things.
I want to toddle back there and
peek over the kitchen counter,
eyes ablaze with excitement
and a willingness to fail.

There must have been lobsters that fell out,
slipped her grip and plunged back into the sea.
Maybe she didn't mind. She could come back tomorrow.
As the years went on, the weight of what she did do
mounting and clattering in the dusk.

Acknowledgments

Grateful acknowledgment of the following publications in which these poems first appeared:

"Object Permanence" appeared in *Alaska Quarterly Review*; "Defensible Space" appeared in *Anacapa Review*; "Death Found Me Like a Knave" appeared in *Anti-Heroin Chic*; "Learning to Pray" appeared in *Braided Way Magazine*; "Life History" appeared in *Crab Creek Review*; "The Scientist and the Poet" appeared in *Consilience Journal*; "Gathering Stones" and "How I Wanted to Be Beautiful" appeared in *Green Shoe Sanctuary*; "After Days of Deep Grief" appeared in *Poetry Breakfast*; "Alterations" appeared in *Spillway Magazine*; "Learning to Fish" and "Every Day, Something New" appeared in *Synkroniciti Magazine*; "Turtles at the *Convention Center*," "The Oldest Lobster Fisher in the World Says She Might as Well Keep Doing It," "Mother's Day," and "Changing the Daisies" appeared in *Thimble Literary Magazine*; "Insights from Arthropods" and "Rorschach Test. Mt Tamalpais" appeared in *Wild Roof Journal*; "The Sparrows (or, Once Again, I Was Wrong)," "A Reckoning with Johnny Appleseed," and "For the Love of Spiders" appeared in *Verse-Virtual*; and "Chrysalis" was commissioned to appear on the wall of a meditation room at the Ohana Center for Child and Adolescent Behavioral Health.

I'm so grateful for my friends, for my communities, for my acquaintances. I really like you all. Often as I'm out for walks or running errands, the memory of some person or another will pop into my mind. *Oh, THAT person!* I'll think. *They're so great! I'm so glad I know them.* So if we're friends or acquaintances, or really, if we've ever met (even if it's been a long time since we've spoken), know that you're probably being thought of by me from time to time with joy and a lot appreciation.

This book (like most books, I think) came into being in community. The community that grew this book was Mahiarishi International University's MFA program. All the guests, teachers, and students I encountered during my time as a student there offered something to my writing process. I thank you.

To my fellow poetry students Kai Black, Antwan Linton Penn, Almedia Stewart, Aliyah Warwick, Elaina Whitesell, Emmy June Breffle, Jessi Elliott, Priya Lin, and Cheryl Michie— thank you for your reflections on these poems and for your own work and wisdom.

To my MFA mentors, thank you for creating an incredibly nurturing community in which to write. Thanks, too, for what you each gave individually: Joshua Jennifer Espinoza, a deep affirmation of my identity; Rustin Larson, wisdom on the revision process and an early and encouraging read of the manuscript; and Eileen Espinoza, support as I embarked upon the submission process and returned to generating new work. Thank you to Candice Rankin for an early read of the manuscript.

A deep and special thank you to Nynke Passi for your vision and dedication. You made the MFA program I'd waited my whole career to attend.

Diane Frank, thanks forever for publishing my first book, for believing in my work, and for connecting me to the school that would become my literary home for two years.

Naomi Shihab Nye, thank you for your friendship, encouragement, and support. Thanks, too, for your poems, which have been my teachers since the first day I met them.

Thank you to more teachers and mentors along the way: Barbara McBride, Pat Robel, Nicole Terez Dutton, Rick Benjamin, Sarah Rabkin, Andie Thrams, Genine Lentine, Tova Green, Prartho Sereno, Danusha Laméris, Farnaz Fatemi, Tehmina Kahn, and James Crews.

The list of authors who have shaped my sensibility as a writer is very long, and I won't attempt to be comprehensive here. The following individuals' work was particularly influential during the writing of this book: Ada Limón, adrienne maree brown, Alberto Ríos, Arthur Dawson, Camille Dungy, Ellery Akers, Felicia Rose Chavez, Jane Hirschfield, Joshua Jennifer Espinoza, Kim Shuck, Kyle Lukoff, Loretta Diane Walker, Lucille Clifton, Molly Fisk, Naomi Shihab Nye, Ocean Vuong, Oliver Bendorf, Pınar Sinopoulos-Lloyd, So Sinopoulos-Lloyd, Rick Benjamin, Robin Wall Kimmerer, William Stafford, W.S. Merwin, and Victoria Chang.

I'm extremely grateful to the extended community of writers and poets with whom I've shared space, written, and swapped support, encouragement, and ideas. My thanks, also, to the many outdoor and environmental educators I've worked alongside or connected with over the years. You have and continue to shape my perspectives on being in relationship with place. Big gratitude to my students for your enthusiasm as we've spent time learning together.

Thank you to my parents, Katherine Heller and Rolf Lygren and my sister, Erika Lygren for cheering on my work as a writer and for your immense love and support. Thank you to Rachel Economy for endless cups of tea and reassuring me when I think I'm doing a bad job at everything.

Thank you to Kevin for your companionship and support, for your love and humor, for the way you fill our lives with community and connection and creativity and whimsy.

Lastly, my deepest gratitude place and places. You were my first teachers. I am forever your student.

About the Author

Emilie Lygren is a nonbinary poet and educator whose work is grounded in curiosity and reverence. She's taught writing in a variety of contexts: classrooms, research stations, graduate programs, parks, libraries, and beyond. Emilie calls on her years of experience as an outdoor educator and curriculum developer to help students connect with themselves, one another, and the places they find themselves in. Emilie's poems have appeared in numerous journals and magazines, including the *Alaska Quarterly Review, Wayfarer Magazine,* and *Crab Creek Poetry Review* (where her poem was a semifinalist for the Crab Creek Poetry Award). Her first book of poetry, *What We Were Born For,* won the Blue Light Book award was chosen by the Young People's Poet Laureate as a monthly book pick from the Poetry Foundation. Emilie is currently an outdoor educator, a professor of creative writing, a poet in the schools, and at work on an anthology of poems on mental health for teens and youth. She lives on Coast Miwok land in San Rafael, California.

Find more of her work and words at emilielygren.com.

At Wayfarer Books we believe poetry is the language of the earth. We believe words—shaped like rivers through wild places—can change the shape of the world. We publish poets and writers and renegades who stand outside of mainstream culture—poets, essayists, and storytellers whose work might withstand the scrutiny of crows and coyotes, those who are cryptic and floral, the crepuscular, and the queer-at-heart. We are more than just a publisher but a community of writers. Our mission is to produce books that can serve as a compass and map to all wayfarers through wild terrain.

wayfarerbooks.org

www.ingramcontent.com/pod-product-compliance
Lightning Source LLC
Chambersburg PA
CBHW031420120626
46545CB00006B/2200